WITHDRAWN

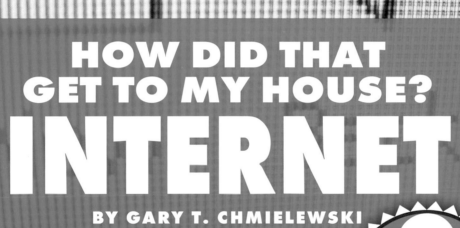

HOW DID THAT GET TO MY HOUSE?

INTERNET

BY GARY T. CHMIELEWSKI

COMMUNITY CONNECTIONS

Published in the United States of America by Cherry Lake Publishing
Ann Arbor, Michigan
www.cherrylakepublishing.com

Content Adviser: Mary Raber, Associate Director, Institute for Interdisciplinary Studies,
Michigan Technological University
Reading Adviser: Cecilia Minden-Cupp, PhD, Literacy Consultant

Photo Credits: Cover and page 1, ©dave jepson/Alamy; page 5, ©Jacek Chabraszewski,
used under license from Shutterstock, Inc.; page 7, ©Scott Rothstein, used under license from
Shutterstock, Inc.; page 9, ©iStockphoto.com/karens4; page 11, ©J Marshall-Tribaleye
Images/Alamy; page 13, ©Danita Delimont/Alamy; page 15, ©iStockphoto.com/Infomages;
page 17, ©Worldspec/NASA/Alamy; page 19, ©iStockphoto.com/AvailableLight; page 21,
©Rob Marmion, used under license from Shutterstock, Inc.

LIBRARY OF CONGRESS CATALOGING-IN-PUBLICATION DATA
Chmielewski, Gary, 1949–
 How did that get to my house? Internet / by Gary T. Chmielewski.
  p. cm.—(Community connections)
 Includes bibliographical references and index.
 ISBN-13: 978-1-60279-477-1
 ISBN-10: 1-60279-477-4
 1. Internet—Juvenile literature. I. Title. II. Title: Internet. III. Series.
 TK5105.875.I57C45 2009
 004.67'8—dc22   2009001196

Cherry Lake Publishing would like to acknowledge the
work of The Partnership for 21st Century Skills. Please
visit *www.21stcenturyskills.org* for more information.

INTERNET

CONTENTS

THE WORLD WIDE WEB

It is late Sunday afternoon. You have a report to finish for school. You need to find some information, but the library is closed. Now what? Do you have a computer? You can still do your homework. The information on the **World Wide Web** can help you.

The Internet can be very helpful for homework.

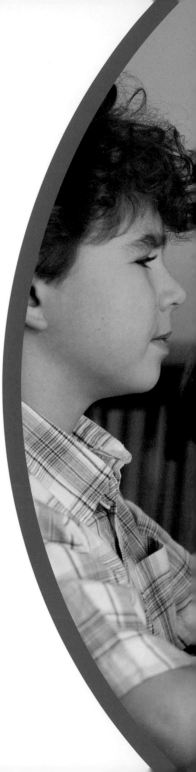

HOW DOES THE INTERNET WORK?

Think about how your home telephone works. The telephone company gives you a phone number. The company also gives you a phone line.
A phone jack connects your telephone to the line. Then you can make and receive calls.

Look at your home phone. Does it have a phone jack like this one that plugs into the wall?

Take a walk with an adult down the block you live on. Do you see any telephone poles? Are there lines running from the poles to the houses? These are telephone lines.

What do phone numbers have to do with connecting to the Internet? An **Internet Service Provider** (ISP) gives you a number. It is called an **Internet Protocol** (IP) **address**. It works kind of like a phone number, but it doesn't connect two telephones. Instead, an IP address lets computers connect with one another.

Ask your mom or dad if you have an Internet Service Provider. If you do, you can connect to the Internet.

Computers on the Internet can share information. Have you visited a Web site? Each Web site has a **Uniform Resource Locator** (URL). URLs look like this: http://www.yahoo.com.

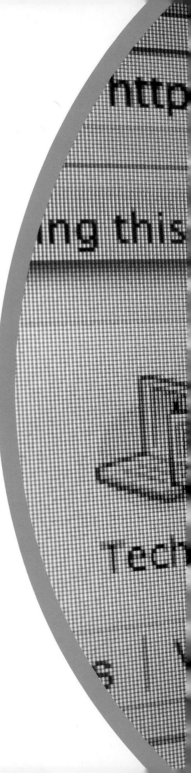

You can usually see a Web site's URL near the top of the screen.

WAYS TO CONNECT

A tool called a modem will connect you to the Internet. It uses your phone line. This is called a dial-up connection. It is slow and takes a long time. Many people prefer to use faster methods.

Modems can be located on the outside or the inside of a computer.

One faster way to connect is through a **digital subscriber line** (DSL). How is DSL different from dial-up? You still need a phone line and a modem, but they are used in a different way. This makes it much faster to send information between computers.

How can you tell this is a DSL modem? Hint: do you see the letters "DSL" anywhere?

DSL

USB

ETHERNET

What kind of Internet connection do you have at home? Is it fast? Ask friends what kind of Internet connections they use. Are they the same or different from the kind you have at home?

15

Cable Internet connections are a lot like DSL. They don't use phone lines though. Cable modems work with the cable lines that carry television programs.

Some people use objects that orbit Earth to connect to the Internet. These objects are called satellites. They are often used by people who can't get DSL or cable connections.

Satellites such as this one help some people connect to the Internet.

Computers don't have to use phone or cable wires. Cell phones and laptop computers connect without using any wires. These types of connections are called wireless, or wi-fi. They use **radio waves** to send and receive information.

Many cell phones can be used to search the Internet.

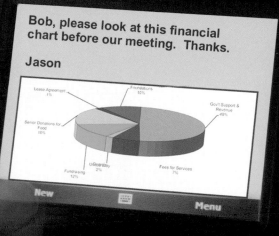

Bob, please look at this financial chart before our meeting. Thanks.

Jason

MAKE A GUESS!

Can you name some places where you can get free wi-fi service? Did you guess hotels, libraries, or coffee shops? If you did, you are correct. Can you name any others?

19

How does the Internet get to your house? Maybe you have a DSL or cable connection. Maybe you have a dial-up connection. It doesn't matter what kind of connection you have. What matters is finishing your homework. Time to get busy!

The Internet is an important part of modern life.

GLOSSARY

cable (KAY-buhl) a bundle of wires that carry signals for telephones, television, and the Internet

digital subscriber line (DIJ-uh-tuhl sub-SRIBE-ur LINE) a way to send information over telephone lines

Internet Protocol address (IN-tur-net PRO-tuh-call ah-DRESS) the set of numbers that identifies your computer to other computers on the Internet

Internet Service Provider (IN-tur-net SUR-viss pro-VYE-dur) a company that connects computers to the Internet

radio waves (RAY-dee-oh WAYVS) invisible waves of energy that carry telephone, TV, and other signals

Uniform Resource Locator (YOO-nuh-form REE-sorss LOH-kay-tor) a Web site's address

World Wide Web (WURLD WIDE WEB) the collection of Web sites and other resources available on the Internet

FIND OUT MORE

BOOKS

Bodden, Valerie. *Internet*. Mankato, MN: Creative Education, 2008.

Oxlade, Chris. *My First Internet Guide*. Chicago: Heinemann Library, 2007.

WEB SITES

Ask Kids
www.askkids.com
Check out this search engine made just for kids

Burlington County Library: Internet for Kids
www.burlco.lib.nj.us/Classes/Intforkids/
Practice your computer skills, and learn more about how to get around the World Wide Web

INDEX

ABOUT THE AUTHOR

Gary Chmielewski is a former library director. His career in children's publishing for the school and library market ranges from purchasing director of a major book wholesaler to executive for a prestigious children's and young adult publisher.